| DATE |  |  |  |
|---|---|---|---|
|  |  |  |  |
|  |  |  |  |
|  |  |  |  |
|  |  |  |  |
|  |  |  |  |
|  |  |  |  |
|  |  |  |  |
|  |  |  |  |
|  |  |  |  |
|  |  |  |  |
|  |  |  |  |

BAKER & TAYLOR BOOKS

# BRUCE LEE'S FIGHTING METHOD

## SELF-DEFENSE TECHNIQUES

by

**Bruce Lee and M. Uyehara**

ISBN No. 0-89750-050-4

**WARNING**

This book is presented only as a means of preserving a unique aspect of the heritage of the martial arts. Neither Ohara Publications nor the author makes any representation, warranty or guarantee that the techniques described or illustrated in this book will be safe or effective in any self-defense situation or otherwise. You may be injured if you apply or train in the techniques of self-defense illustrated in this book, and neither Ohara Publications nor the author is responsible for any such injury that may result. It is essential that you consult a physician regarding whether or not to attempt any technique described in this book. Specific self-defense responses illustrated in this book may not be justified in any particular situation in view of all of the circumstances or under the applicable federal, state or local law. Neither Ohara Publications nor the author makes any representation or warranty regarding the legality or appropriateness of any technique mentioned in this book.

OHARA ⬛ PUBLICATIONS, INCORPORATED

SANTA CLARITA, CALIFORNIA

## DEDICATION

To all the friends and students of Bruce Lee

## ACKNOWLEDGEMENT

Our sincere appreciation to Joe Bodner, who spent so much time in photographing and developing the films. Our appreciation also goes to those who participated in these books: Dan Inosanto, Ted Wong and Raymond Huang. They were all Bruce Lee's devoted students.

# INTRODUCTION

This book was in the making in 1966 and most of the photographs were shot then. The late Bruce Lee intended to publish this book years ago but decided against it when he learned that martial arts instructors were using his name to promote themselves. It was quite common to hear comments like: "I taught Bruce Lee" or "Bruce Lee taught me jeet kune do." And Bruce may never have seen or known these martial artists.

Bruce didn't want people to use his name to promote themselves or their schools with false pretenses. He didn't want them to attract students this way, especially the young teens.

But after his death, his widow, Linda, felt that Bruce had contributed so much in the world of the martial arts that it would be a great loss if the knowledge of Bruce would die with him. Although the book can never replace the actual teaching and knowledge that Bruce Lee possessed, it will enhance you, the serious martial artist, in developing your skill in fighting.

Bruce always believed that all martial artists train diligently for one single purpose—to defend themselves. Whether we are in judo,

karate, aikido, kung fu, etcetera, our ultimate goal is to prepare ourselves for any situation.

To train yourself for this goal, you must train seriously. Nothing is taken for granted. "You have to kick or punch the bag with concentrated efforts," Bruce used to say. "If you are going to train without the concept that this is the real thing, you are short-changing yourself. When you kick or punch the bag, you have to imagine that you are actually hitting an adversary. Really concentrating, putting 100 percent in your kicks and punches, is the only way you are going to be good."

In order to understand this book more clearly, you should also read two other books to be published in the future. One is Bruce Lee's basic training methods, and the other is a thorough application of his techniques. Most of the photos in this book and the next two have never been published before.

If you have not read *Tao of Jeet Kune Do* by Bruce Lee (Ohara Publications, Inc.), please read it. It was meant to complement this book, and the knowledge from both books will give you a full picture of Bruce's art.

# CONTENTS

CHAPTER I

# DEFENSE AGAINST SURPRISE ATTACK

The best defense against a surprise attack is not to be "surprised." In other words, Bruce Lee always emphasized that a martial artist must constantly be aware of his surroundings. He must be trained to be cautious and alert at all times. He should never be caught napping before an attack.

In the following segments of self-defense, you will quickly notice that most of the attacks against Lee are prevented because of his alertness.

Lee attempted here to enact a practical condition that could occur to anyone in his daily life. He always believed that the best defense is to be quicker than your assailant.

But to do this, you must practice constantly. All techniques must be done fluidly and with power and swiftness.

## ATTACK FROM THE SIDE

(1&2) Walking down the street, Lee noticed some-one standing at the corner. Instead of walking nearby him, he leaves enough room for himself to defend against an ambush. (3&4) As the assailant attacks, Lee counters with a quick and powerful side kick to the forward knee. (5) The kick is followed through completely so that it causes the assailant to reel back-

ward. (6) Lee counterattacks with multiple hooking and straight punches to the face, keeping the assailant off-balance.

*COMMENT: You constantly have to practice the side kick on a heavy bag—preferably about 70 lbs.—to develop good power. Notice that Lee delivers his kick by keeping his body away from the assailant.*

## ATTACK WHILE ENTERING A CAR

(1) As Lee attempts to enter his car, he is aware of the assailant. (2&3) As the assailant attempts to kick, Lee surprises him by countering with a side kick to the knee. (4&5) The kick drops the assailant to the ground. (6) Lee follows up with a hooking kick to the head.

*COMMENT: It seems the assailant has a step on Lee, but*

anyone who has seen Lee's performance knows how fast he was. Lee is able to counter with a kick because his movement is fluid and quick. To be this quick, you have to practice kicking in the air with speed or hitting a light bag. Don't kick hard while practicing this, as you may hurt your knees. Solid kicks should be done on a heavy bag.

## AMBUSH FROM THE REAR

(1—3) The assailant follows from the rear, but Lee is aware of him and pretends he doesn't see him. (4—6) Before the assailant can throw a punch, Lee counters with a side or back kick to assailant's knee, knocking him backward. (7&8) Lee

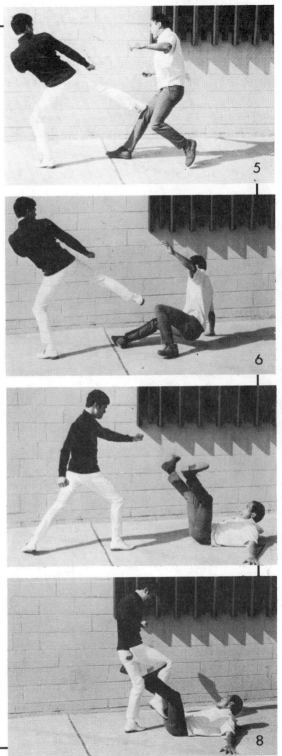

follows up by turning to execute a groin kick.

*COMMENT: If Lee had turned around to face the assailant, he would give the assailant an added advantage of preparing his attack. By being a wary decoy, he allows himself this added advantage.*

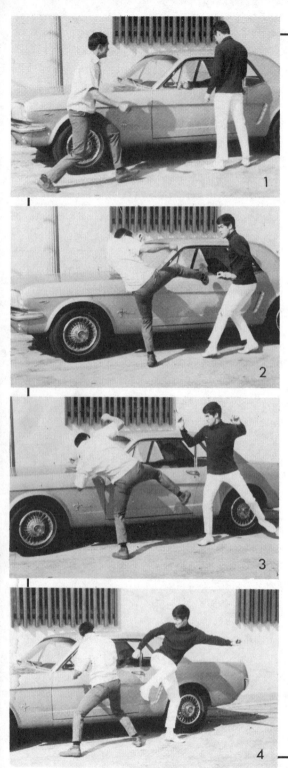

## AMBUSH AT CLOSE QUARTERS

(1&2) As Lee prepares to enter his car, the assailant rushes toward him and attempts a kick to his midsection. (3) Lee steps back. (4—6) As soon as the assailant places his foot down,

Lee executes his side kick to the back of the assailant's knee. (7&8) He quickly follows up with a choke hold.

5

6

7

8

CHAPTER II

# DEFENSE AGAINST AN UNARMED ASSAILANT

Bruce Lee demonstrates how to handle the several different forms of assault in this chapter. For years he kept saying that you are wasting a lot of energy and even making yourself less effective by studying "set patterns" (kata). To him, "fighting is simple and total."

In this chapter, some of the approaches by the attacker may seem irrational. But, as Lee himself said, "There are many irrational people on the street today."

## DEFENSE AGAINST A CROUCHING ATTACK

(1) The assailant approaches Lee in a crouch, an unusual way of attacking. (2—4) From a southpaw stance, Lee delivers a side kick to the side of the forward knee, causing the assailant to drop. (5—8) Lee then follows through by dragging the assailant backward by his shirt collar and finishes him off with a heel stomp to the face.

*COMMENT: Lee includes this in his self-defense series because some schools of martial arts do not prepare the students for situations like this. Besides, some schools will teach their students to stop after the opponent is down, but Lee always felt that the assailant is trying to maim or kill you so you have to be sure he can't retaliate.*

## DEFENSE AGAINST A REVERSE PUNCH

In this bird's-eye view, Lee shows how an attack can be nullified by a simple maneuver. (1&2) As the assailant moves forward to attempt a right punch, Lee delivers a side kick to his groin (3) with his forward foot.

*COMMENT: Many karate schools teach their students to block once or several times before countering. Lee believes that it is more effective to counter immediately, as he has done here. But to do this, you must be quicker than the attacker.*

## DEFENSE AGAINST A FULL SWING

(1) Against a full swing, Lee has more time to counter because the assailant greatly telegraphs his movement. (2&3) Before the punch can reach him, Lee puts his weight on his rear leg and executes a side kick to the chest.

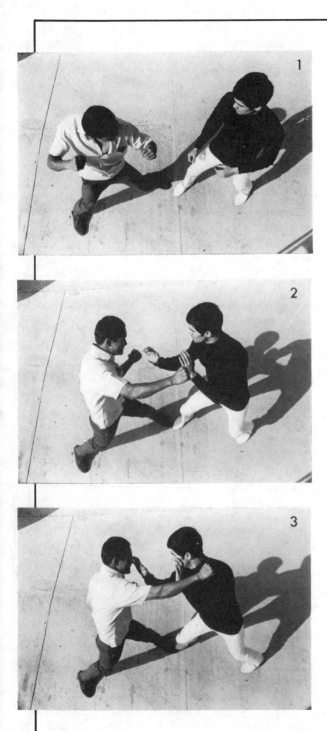

## DEFENSE AGAINST
## A HOOKING PUNCH, No. 1

(1 & 2) In this view from above, we see the assailant attack Lee with an attempted right hook. Lee parries the block to the side of his head and (3) immediately follows with a finger jab to the eyes.

## DEFENSE AGAINST A HOOKING PUNCH, No. 2

(1&2) As the assailant attempts a right hook, Lee rotates his hips clockwise, quickly placing his weight evenly on both feet and (3) executes a finger jab to the eyes without blocking the attack. Lee's striking hand and change of position cause the assailant's punch to miss its mark.

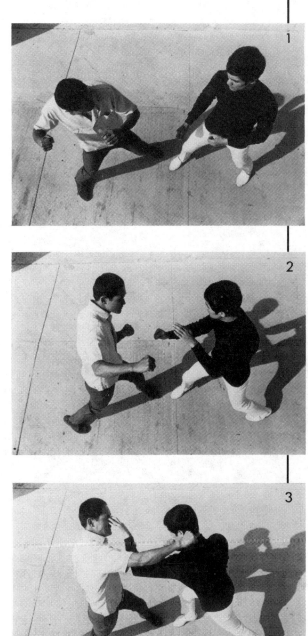

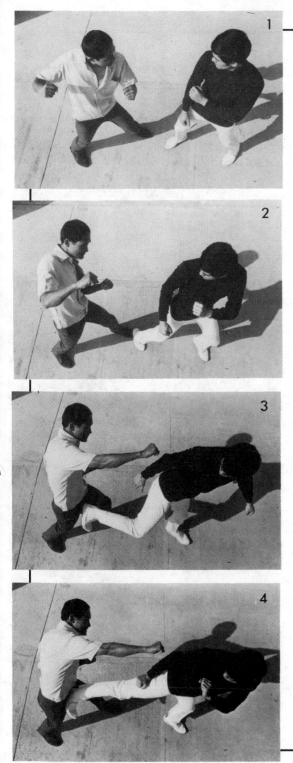

## DEFENSE AGAINST A HOOKING PUNCH, No. 3

(1 & 2) As the assailant attempts a right hook, Lee rotates his hip, placing most of his weight on his rear foot and (3 & 4) counters with a side kick to the groin, using his forward foot.

COMMENT: *In the case of the roundhouse punch, Lee has more time because the blow is telegraphed, so he can counter with a side kick, stepping away from the blow before delivering the kick. In defense against the hooking punch, Lee demonstrates two variations of the finger jab counterattack. Bruce personally preferred the latter of these two because of the economy of movement. (This is the wing chun "inner gate" jab, which can be seen on page 124 of* Wing Chun *by J. Yimm Lee).*

## DEFENSE AGAINST A TACKLE, No. 1

(1—3) Like the full-swing attack, Lee has more time to counter against someone trying to tackle him. As the assailant attempts to tackle him, he steps back and delivers a front kick to his face.

29

## DEFENSE AGAINST A TACKLE, No. 2

(1 & 2) As assailant attempts to tackle Lee, he just steps back (3—5), grabs the assailant's hair and hand, and pulls him to the ground. (6—8) He then uses the attacker's own momentum to turn him over so he can stomp his face (9).

*COMMENT: Lee always felt that self-defense means that you do anything to get out of a situation or use any way to defend yourself. He normally would not have used the hair tactic in a real fight but he was trying to tell you that it could be effective, too.*

2

3

5

6

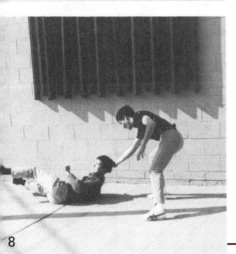

8

9

## DEFENSE AGAINST A TACKLE, No. 3

(1&2) As the assailant attacks, slide your rear foot back slightly to brace yourself. (3&4) Grab the assailant's neck in a headlock as he comes toward you. (5&6) Slide your front

foot backward and pin the assailant to the ground while maintaining a choke hold. Be sure to execute the pin quickly or the attacker could make a strike to your groin.

4

5

6

## CHAPTER III

# DEFENSE AGAINST GRABBING

When an assailant grabs you, he usually has the jump on you. But it doesn't mean he has the advantage, because he doesn't know how you will retaliate.

When you are seized in close quarters, your most practical defense is in your hands. You are too close to deliver an effective kick. But a kick can be delivered if the assailant leaves enough distance between you and him. For instance, if he grabs your wrist, you have room for a shin or knee kick.

## DEFENSE AGAINST A CHEST GRAB

(1&2) The assailant seizes Lee's chest with his left hand and attempts to knee his groin. Lee blocks his knee with his left hand and in one motion (3&4) grabs the assailant's left hand and simultaneously executes a right bottom fist strike to his groin. (5—7) Then he thrusts his left hand to the assailant's throat and shoves him backward to the ground. (8&9) Lee jumps high and places a well-timed stomp on the assailant's face.

*COMMENT: You have to practice this technique over and over again to do it effectively, as there are so many movements involved. On photos 5 to 7, you cannot drop your assailant down unless you use one hand to shove the throat while the other hand is used as a lever, grabbing the assailant's sleeve and pulling it clockwise and downward.*

4

7

## DEFENSE AGAINST
## AN ARM GRAB, No. 1

(1) With both hands, the assailant grabs Lee's arm. (2&3) Lee quickly faces him and delivers a low crescent kick to the knee followed by a punch to the face (4) and a left

front kick to his groin (5).

COMMENT: *The crescent kick may not be powerful when you first attempt it, but constant practice can make it into a valuable and strong kick.*

## DEFENSE AGAINST
## AN ARM GRAB, No. 2

(1) The assailant grabs Lee's arm with both hands. (2 & 3) Without unnecessary motion, Lee delivers a side kick to the assailant's knee.

## DEFENSE AGAINST
## AN ARM GRAB, No. 3

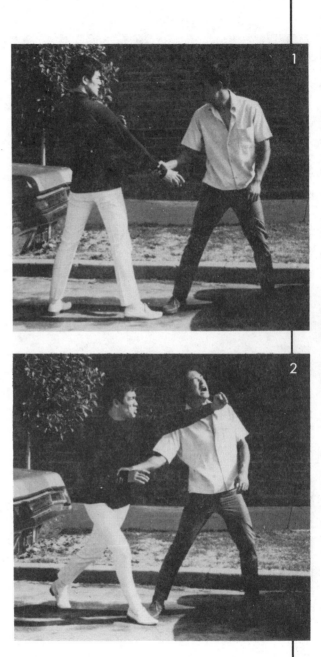

(1) The assailant grabs Lee's right wrist. (2) Before assailant can throw his punch, Lee counters with a left cross.

*COMMENT: Sometimes a martial arts instructor teaches his student several motions to dispose of an assailant, when it could be done with just a simple blow, as in the above sequences.*

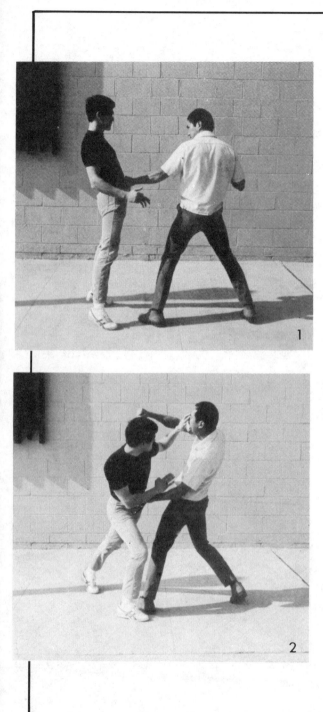

## DEFENSE AGAINST
## A BELT HOLD

(1) The assailant grabs Lee's belt and pulls toward him. (2) Because he is too close for a kicking technique, Lee leans away from the attacker's punch and simultaneously executes a finger jab to the eyes.

## DEFENSE AGAINST A WRISTLOCK

(1) The assailant puts a wristlock on Lee with both hands. (2&3) Lee quickly turns clockwise and executes a reverse elbow strike.

*COMMENT: Bruce Lee always emphasized that you don't turn your back to your opponent, but in this case, it was done quickly enough to be effective.*

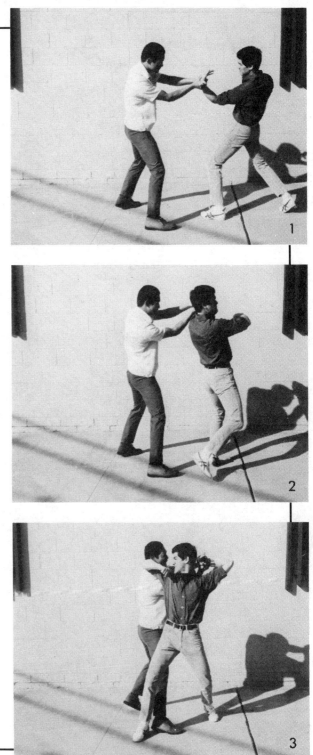

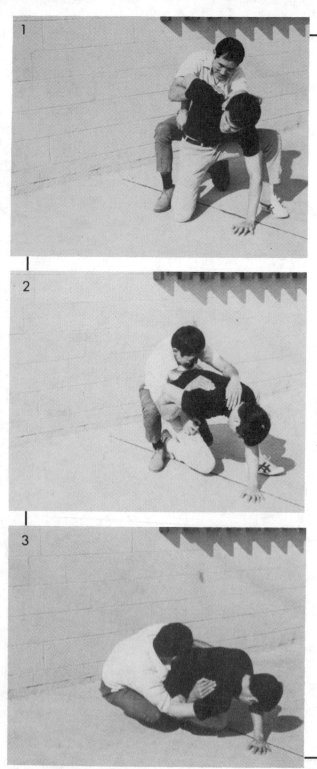

## DEFENSE AGAINST A HALF NELSON

(1 & 2) Attacking Lee from behind, the assailant locks his right arm and keeps his head in a grip. (3&4) Using the attacking momentum, Lee turns his body toward his

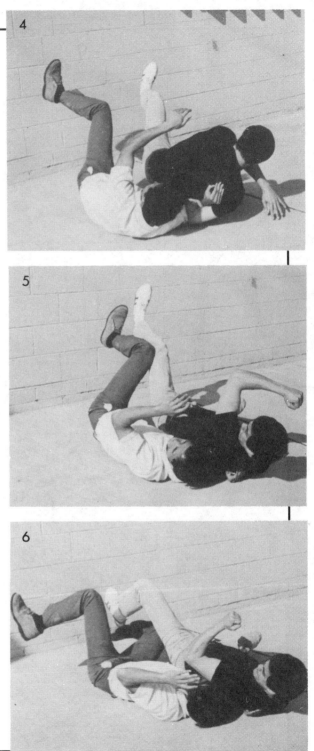

locked arm (counter-clockwise), forcing the assailant off-balance. (5&6) Keeping the assailant's arm locked under his body, he delivers a reverse elbow strike.

## DEFENSE AGAINST
## A REVERSE WRISTLOCK

(1&2) The assailant puts a reverse wristlock on Lee's right hand. (3) Lee retaliates with a side kick to his midsection and (4&5) a spinning back kick to the same section

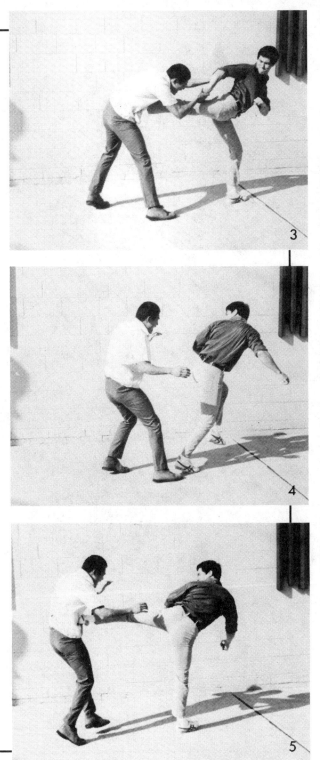

with his other foot.

COMMENT: *When someone grabs you with a reverse lock as in photos 2&3, you have to counter quickly before he can pin you to the ground.*

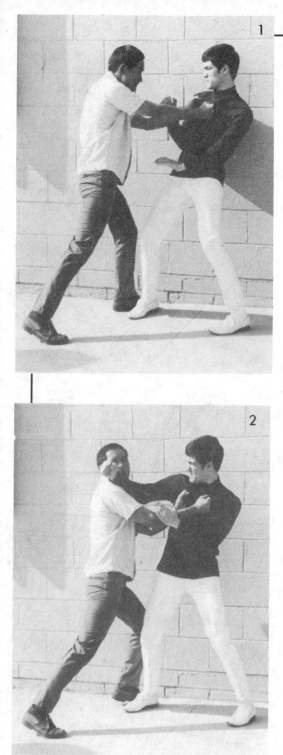

## DEFENSE AGAINST A
## TWO-HAND CHEST GRAB, No. 1

(1) The assailant grabs Lee's chest with both hands. Note that Lee uses his left hand to protect his groin. (2) Lee lifts the same hand to lock his assailant's arm while simultaneously executing a right cross to his face.

## DEFENSE AGAINST A TWO-HAND CHEST GRAB, No. 2

(1) The assailant grabs Lee's chest with both hands. Note that Lee uses his left hand to protect his groin. (2) Lee lifts the same hand to lock his assailant's arm. He follows with a forward elbow strike to the helpless assailant's face.

*COMMENT: The important maneuver in this section is to trap the assailant's right hand and attack before he can do damage to you.*

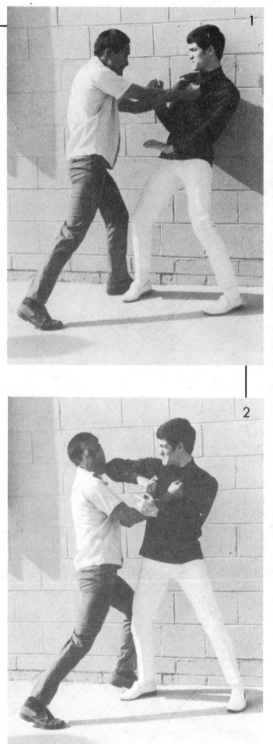

## DEFENSE AGAINST
## A SHOULDER GRAB
## FROM THE REAR

(1) The assailant grabs Lee's shoulder from the rear. (2&3) Lee turns his torso and applies a backfist punch to the assailant's face.

*COMMENT: To have power in your backfist punch, you have to step back slightly and apply the punch by simultaneously rotating your hip.*

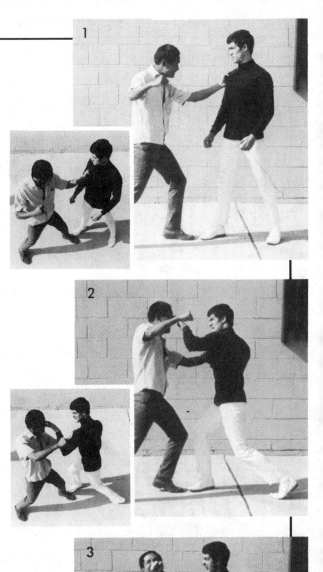

## DEFENSE AGAINST A ONE-HAND CHEST GRAB

(1) The assailant grabs Lee's chest with his left hand and delivers a right swing toward Lee's face. (2&3) Lee doesn't even bother to block, but applies a straight inner finger jab to assailant's eyes and follows up by immobilizing assailant's hand and simultaneously hitting him with a right uppercut.

*COMMENT: Finger-jabbing simultaneously against a swing looks easy, but it isn't. You have to practice this constantly to get it right. This technique comes from wing chun kung fu. (See page 124,* Wing Chun *by J. Yimm Lee.)*

51

## DEFENSE AGAINST
## A HIGH REVERSE WRISTLOCK

(1&2) The assailant applies a high reverse wristlock to your left hand. (3&4) Turn clockwise and apply a back kick.

*COMMENT: It isn't common for someone to catch you in a reversed wristlock, but in case it does happen, you should be ready.*

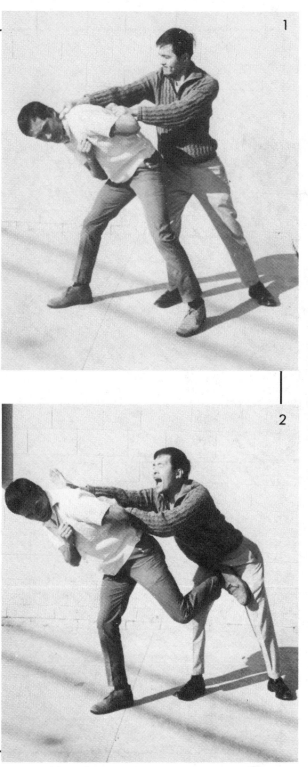

## DEFENSE AGAINST
## A BACK ARM LOCK

(1) The assailant grabs you with a back arm lock that is difficult to get out of. (2) The quickest way is to execute a back kick to his groin.

*COMMENT: Sometimes a knowledgeable assailant will place his foot and body close to you so you can't retaliate with a kick. In this case, you can always maneuver your body so there's enough space to deliver it.*

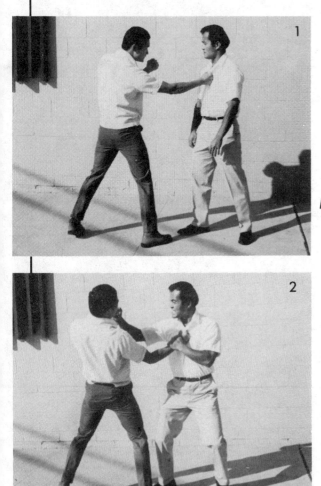

## DEFENSE AGAINST
## A CHEST GRAB AND A PUNCH

(1) The assailant grabs your chest and attempts to punch your face. (2) Grab the assailant's wrist with your left hand and at the same time deliver a punch to his jaw.

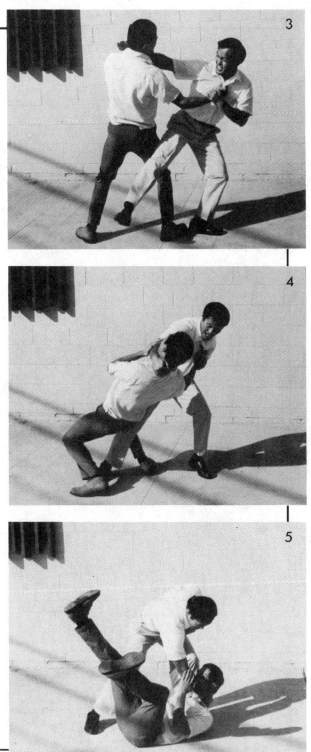

**(3—5)** Follow up with a foot throw.

*COMMENT: Instead of a punch to assailant's jaw, a finger jab will be just as effective. After dropping the assailant, you can also hit him with your hand or foot.*

CHAPTER IV

# DEFENDING AGAINST CHOKE HOLDS AND HUGS

A good martial artist is always alert and should never be surprised. The following self-defense techniques are in situations where you are being surprised and must free yourself from a choke or a hug.

Bruce Lee always explained that the best defense is the most simple and effective—especially against the choke. Lee demonstrates how you can escape and retaliate by direct and simple counters.

In this section he also demonstrates the use of elbows, the head and strikes to the groin.

1

2

3

## DEFENSE AGAINST
## A FRONT CHOKE, No. 1

(1) The assailant chokes Lee, who seizes the assailant's wrist to relieve the pressure on his neck. (2&3) Maintaining his safety grip with one hand, Lee quickly finger-jabs his eyes and follows up (4&5) with a knee to his groin.

*COMMENT: Lee doesn't waste time in his action here. Instead of trying to break the grip first, he counters directly. Notice Lee's right foot touching the assailant's right. This is to prevent the assailant from kicking or kneeing him.*

4

5

## DEFENSE AGAINST
## A FRONT CHOKE, No. 2

(1) The assailant chokes Lee and drives him against the wall. (2) Lee steps out to the side and delivers a front kick to his groin.

*COMMENT: As assailant chokes him, Lee, in this case, is able to get out of the choke and move slightly back, far enough for a front kick.*

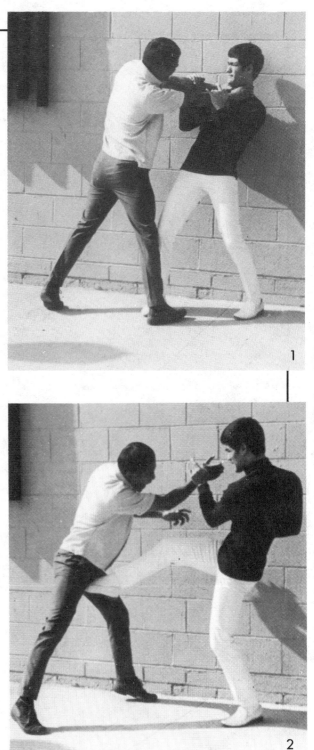

1

2

## DEFENSE AGAINST A HEADLOCK, No. 1

(1) The assailant has a headlock on Lee. (2&3) Lee quickly retaliates with a finger jab to his eyes with his free hand.

## DEFENSE AGAINST A HEADLOCK, No. 2

(1) The assailant has a headlock on Lee. (2&3) Lee is able to place his right hand over the assailant's shoulder and claw his face.

## DEFENSE AGAINST A HEADLOCK, No. 3

(1) The assailant has a headlock on Lee. (2&3) Lee turns his body close to the assailant and with his free hand pounds the assailant's groin.

*COMMENT: Whenever you are caught in a headlock, you must act fast with a counter or else the assailant will drag you to the ground, making it harder to free yourself.*

## DEFENSE AGAINST
## A REAR STRANGLEHOLD

(1) The assailant strangles Lee from the rear and also seizes his right hand. (2) Lee moves slightly to his right and applies a left elbow strike to the assailant's ribs.

*COMMENT: The assailant is really trying to strangle Lee and bend his body backward, but Lee moves to the right before he is in that vulnerable position and has a clean shot at the exposed rib area.*

## DEFENSE AGAINST A BEAR HUG
### (Arms pinned)

(1) The assailant has a bear hug on Lee. (2) To get out of this, Lee steps his right foot out, drops his weight down slightly to loosen the assailant's grip and executes a left hand strike to his groin.

*COMMENT: You can do this maneuver only by constant practice, as there are several coordinated moves you have to do in a split second. This is especially true if the assailant is a strong person.*

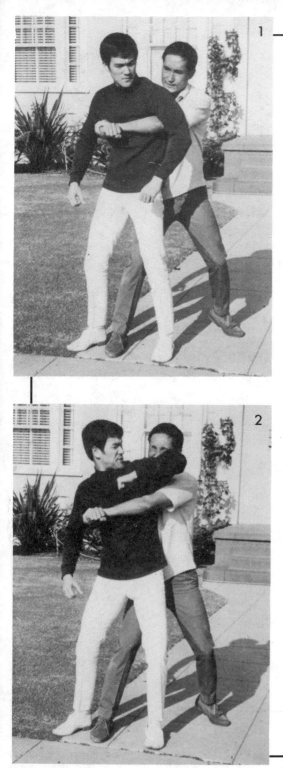

## DEFENSE AGAINST A BEAR HUG
### (Arms free)

(1) The assailant has a bear hug on Lee, but his arms are free. (2) Instead of attempting to free himself from the grip, Lee just delivers a reverse elbow strike to his face.

*COMMENT: In delivering the blow with your elbow, use your hip rotation for added power.*

## DEFENSE AGAINST
## A LIFTING FRONT BEAR HUG

(1) The assailant grabs you from the front and lifts you off your feet. (2—4) Swing your foot back and deliver an upward knee blow to the assailant's groin.

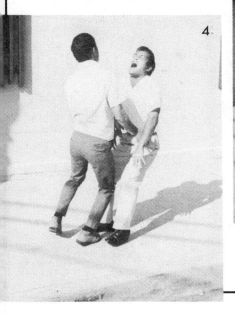

## DEFENSE AGAINST
## A LIFTING REAR BEAR HUG

(1) The assailant grabs you from the rear and lifts you off your feet. (2) Swing back your head to bang it against the assailant's face.

*COMMENT: For the front bear hug, you do have a second or third chance in case you miss the groin, because the assailant can't do anything to you as long as he keeps hugging you. But for the rear bear hug, you do take a risk of getting your head cut open, but in that case the assailant will sustain injury also.*

## DEFENSE AGAINST
## A FRONT HEADLOCK

(1) The assailant has a frontal headlock on you. (2) Before he can drop you to the ground, take aim and punch his groin.

*COMMENT: Sometimes, in close-quarters fighting, you may end up in a headlock. The most important thing is to counter quickly so you are not pinned to the ground.*

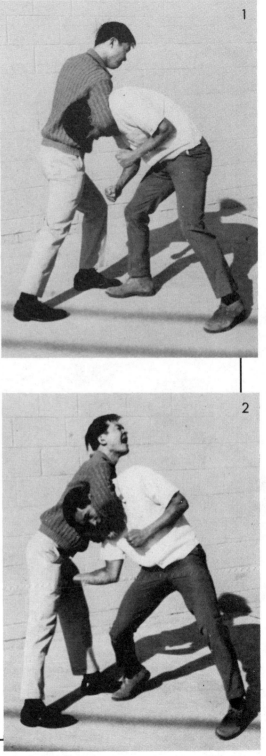

CHAPTER V

# SELF-DEFENSE AGAINST AN ARMED ASSAILANT

Defending against an unarmed assailant is quite a bit different from facing someone with a knife or gun. If you practice self-defense against someone using a "toy" weapon or a facsimile of a weapon, you may perform with proficiency. But try facing a real gun or knife for the first time; you'll have chills down your back or even "freeze" when you know one slip may mean death.

Only constant practice can give you the feeling of comfort or confidence, but even then, it is not a street condition. Going against a club and staff is not as frightening as against a real dagger or gun.

The most dangerous weapon, naturally, is the gun. An assailant wielding a club, knife or staff will telegraph his movement but with a gun, just a little squeeze of the trigger is all you're going to notice.

Bruce Lee demonstrates some of the techniques against an armed assailant but he, himself, always emphasized, "You are at a disadvantage against someone with a weapon, so keep away from him."

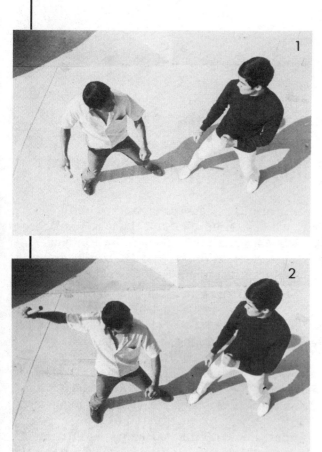

## DEFENSE AGAINST
## A CLUB, No. 1

(1 & 2) The assailan
swings a club at Lee
(3—5) Stepping back jus
enough to let the clut

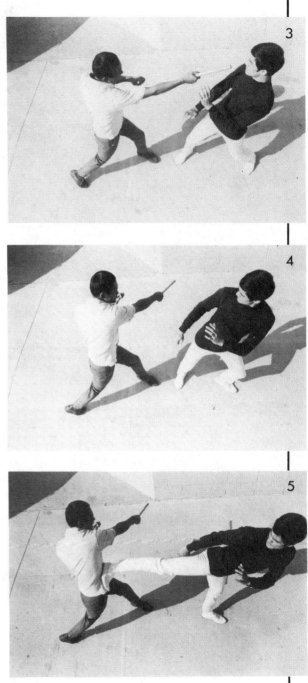

miss him, Lee then retaliates with a side kick to the assailant's body.

1

2

## DEFENSE AGAINST A CLUB, No. 2

(1 & 2) The assailant swings his club at Lee, who ducks under the blow. (3) Lee then grabs the sleeve of the assailant, forcing him downward. (4) He immediately counters with a knee to the face.

3

4

## DEFENSE AGAINST A CLUB, No. 3

(1) The assailant, with both hands on the club, jabs at Lee's midsection. (2) Lee blocks the jab and moves his hips to the side before applying a finger jab to the assailant's eyes.

*COMMENT: Against a club or a lead pipe, you must have good timing and know your distance. One slip and you may be in grave danger, as you are not given a second chance in most instances. Practice is everything.*

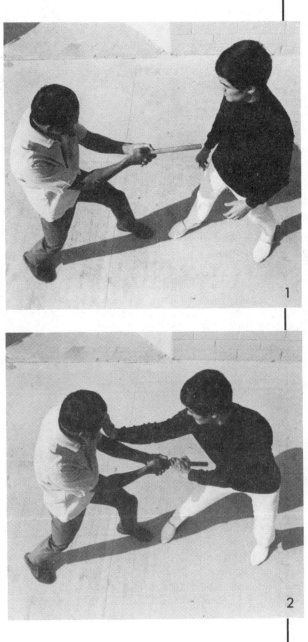

1

## DEFENSE AGAINST A STAFF - JAMMING

(1) The assailant attempts to swing a staff at Lee. (2&3) Lee moves swiftly toward the assailant and jams the assailant's arm with his left hand, simultaneouly punching his body with his right. (4&5) Holding on to the assailant's arm, Lee applies a crescent kick to the ankle that causes the assailant to fall. (6) Lee punches him as he is falling and finishes him off with a rib stomp (7&8).

3

6

## DEFENSE AGAINST
## A STAFF - DUCKING

(1—3) The assailant swings the staff toward Lee, who quickly ducks underneath it. (4&5) As soon as the staff passes his head, Lee quickly counters with a round-house kick to assailant's groin.

3

4

5

## DEFENSE AGAINST
## A STAFF - ELUDING, No. 1

(1 & 2) The assailant swings the staff at Lee, who moves back just enough to elude the blow. (3) As soon as the

blow passes him, Lee moves in quickly with a roundhouse kick to the assailant's head.

## DEFENSE AGAINST
## A STAFF - ELUDING, No. 2

(1—3) The assailant swings the staff at Lee, who moves back to elude the blow. (4&5) As soon as the blow passes him by, he jumps in swiftly and applies a reversed hook or sweeping kick to the assailant's face (6).

## DEFENSE AGAINST
## A STAFF - THRUSTING, No. 1

(1 & 2) The assailant thrusts the staff at Lee's midsection. Lee side-steps the thrust and seizes the staff. (3) He

follows up with a side kick to the assailant's chest, still holding the staff.

2

3

## DEFENSE AGAINST A STAFF - THRUSTING, No. 2

(1 & 2) The assailant thrusts the staff at Lee's midsection. Lee side-steps the thrust and seizes the staff. (3) He then applies a front kick to assailant's arm.

*COMMENT: Against a staff or bo, you have one advantage in that the assailant cannot hide his weapon, and he telegraphs his movement more so than with a club or knife. The disadvantage to you is that he has a longer reach. He can hit you from further away. It is so important that you do not misjudge in closing the distance. Timing is also important in defending against a staff.*

2

3

## DEFENSE AGAINST
## A KNIFE - GRAB & STAB

(1 & 2) The assailant grabs Lee's shirt and attempts to stab him with a knife. Lee quickly seizes the assailant's left hand, and (3) swings his right arm into the assailant's elbow. (4) Lee simultane-

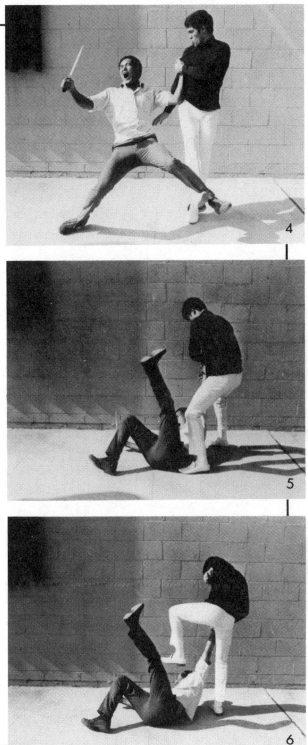

ously trips him with a right foot sweep. (5&6) As soon as the assailant falls to the ground, Lee follows up with a crushing foot thrust to the assailant's body.

4

5

6

## DEFENSE AGAINST
## A KNIFE - THRUST, No. 1

(1&2) Lee faces an assailant with a knife. Before he attacks, Lee fakes a finger jab toward the assailant's face, which causes him to react. (3) At that instant, Lee kicks him in the ankle, leaving enough space between the assailant and himself in applying the kick.

## DEFENSE AGAINST A KNIFE - THRUST, No. 2

(1) The assailant approaches Lee with a knife. (2&3) Lee applies a crescent kick to the assailant's wrist, causing him to drop the knife.

## DEFENSE AGAINST
## A KNIFE - SWING

(1&2) You are "face to face" with an assailant wielding a knife. As he swings the knife at you, you quickly evade the assault by stepping back. (3&4) The instant you see an opening after the knife passes, you move forward and apply a side kick to the back of the assailant's knee, crushing him to the ground.

COMMENT: Facing a person with a knife is quite frightening unless you have actually, mentally prepared for this type of situation from time to time. If you haven't, you should start right away. Should you meet someone with a knife someday, you don't want to "freeze" at that moment. Caution: Always avoid an encounter with an armed person if you possibly can.

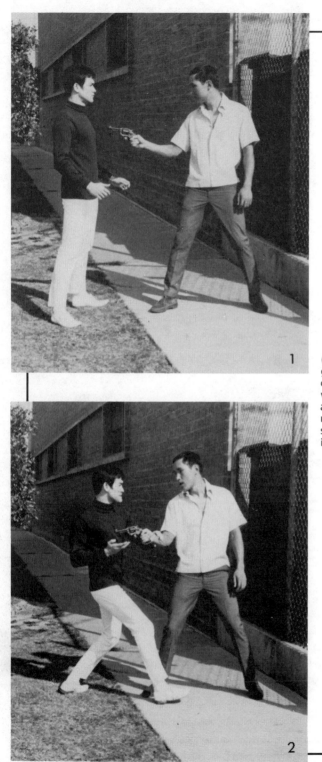

## DEFENSE AGAINST
## A GUN · FRONTAL

(1) The assailant holds a gun at Lee. (2) Lee reacts quickly by stepping forward, twisting his hip and simultaneously parrying and seizing the assailant's wrist so he is not in the line of fire.

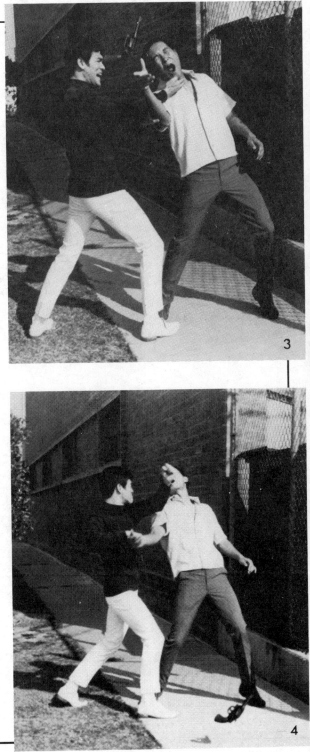

(3&4) With his free hand, Lee attacks the assailant's throat, then slides his hand until he seizes the assailant's wrist and follows up with a left backfist punch.

3

4

## DEFENSE AGAINST
## A GUN - REAR

(1) Assailant points a gun at Lee's back. (2) Lee retaliates by turning his body counterclockwise, using his arm to parry the assailant's hand so he'll be away from the line of fire. (3&4) Then he seizes the assailant's wrist and attacks the throat with his free hand. He follows up with multiple blows to the head.

*COMMENT: As mentioned*

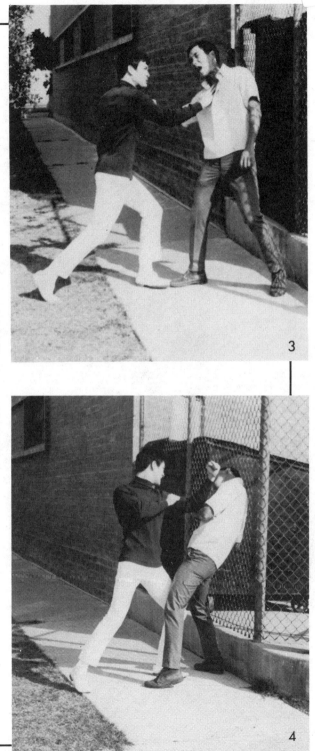

before, taking a gun away
from a person is very risky.
There's no way of taking
away a gun from a distance.
Before you can even reach
the assailant, he has only to
squeeze the trigger a fraction
of a second before the gun
fires. The only chance you'll
ever have against a gun is at
close quarters. Even then it
is difficult, and you can't
make a mistake, as there's no
second chance.

3

4

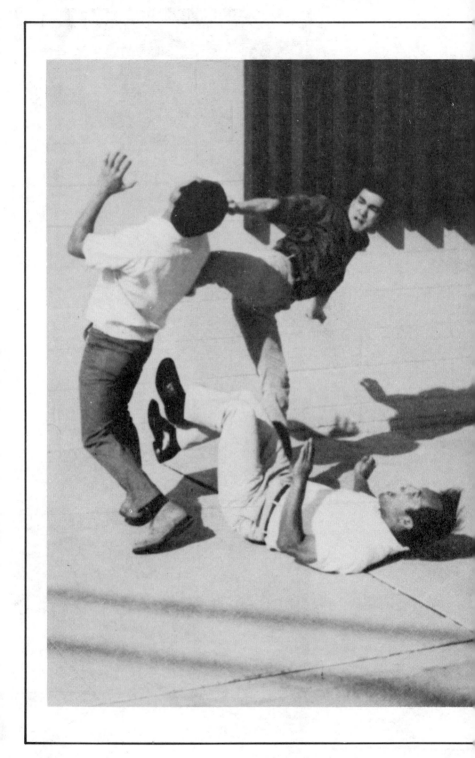

## CHAPTER VI

# DEFENSE AGAINST MULTIPLE ASSAILANTS

If you are attacked by two or more assailants, you may not be in a real disadvantageous position if you are better prepared in fighting than your assailants. Although Bruce Lee explained that he took the unorthodox or "southpaw" stance in his fighting so he could depend mostly on his right foot and hand, you must be able to use both your left and right proficiently against a multiple attack.

Naturally, defending against multiple assailants is harder than against an individual because you have to be cognizant of all your assailants' positions. If you are pinned by two or more individuals, the odds of freeing yourself are heavily against you. Their combined strength and weight may be twice as much as yours.

## DEFENSE AGAINST A REAR AND FRONTAL ATTACK

(1) Assailant **A** pins Lee's left hand behind his back and holds his shirt from the rear. (2) Assailant **B** throws a right punch to his face. (3) Lee ducks the blow, whirls toward his right, freeing his arm

from assailant **A** and applies a backfist punch to his ribs. (4) He then finger-jabs assailant **B**'s throat and (5&6) finishes off assailant **A** with a high side kick.

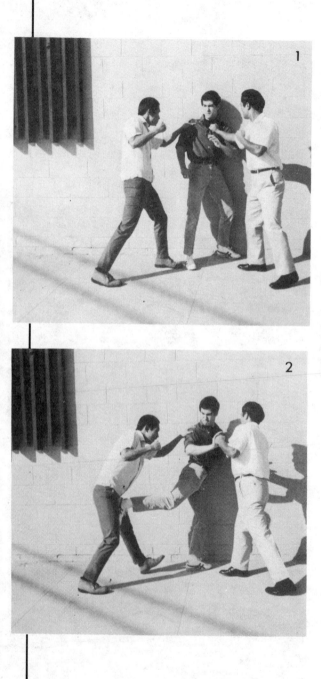

## DEFENSE AGAINST ASSAILANTS AFTER BEING PINNED TO THE WALL

(1) Lee is pinned to the wall by two assailants. (2) He quickly delivers a side kick to the groin of assailant **A** and blocks

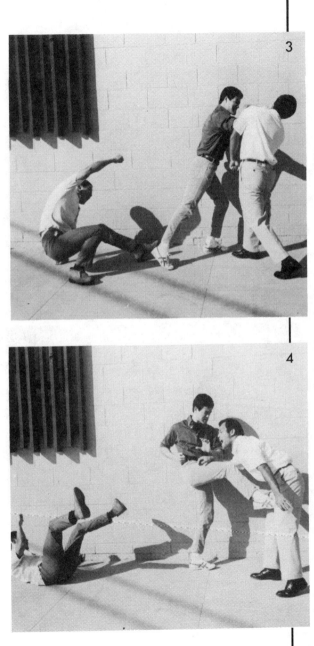

the straight left thrown by assailant **B**. (3&4) He follows up with a right cross and a front kick to the groin of assailant **B**.

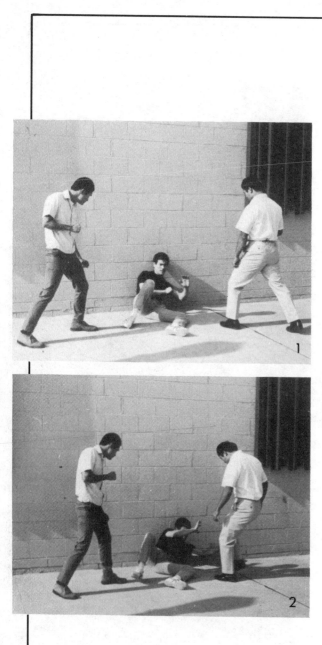

## DEFENSE AGAINST ASSAILANTS FROM A LYING POSITION

(1) While lying on the ground, Lee is attacked by assailants from both directions. (2&3) Lee, using his hands, stops the kick thrown by assailant B, and simultaneously

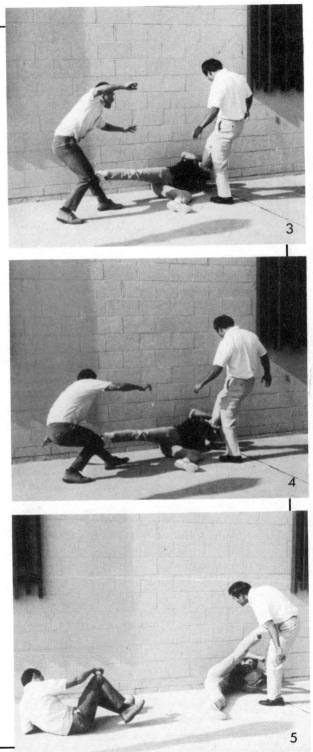

applies a thrust kick to assailant **A**'s knee, toppling him to the ground. (4&5) Hanging on to assailant **B**'s foot, he then applies a forward kick to his groin.

## DEFENSE AGAINST AN AMBUSH FROM ASSAILANTS

(1 & 2) As Lee strolls along, he is stopped by assailant B. (3—5) Lee grabs his wrist, finger-jabs his eyes and follows up with a hook to his chin which sends the assailant tumbling to the ground in front of him. (6 & 7) When assailant A comes to the aid of his fallen comrade, Lee greets him with a hook kick to his chest.

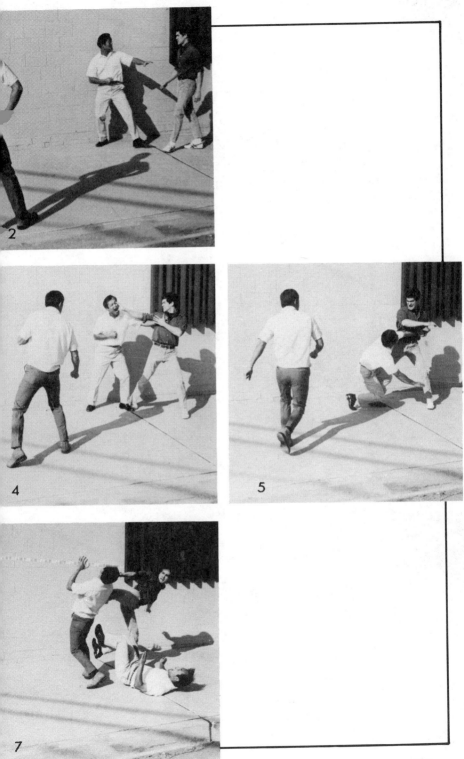

## DEFENSE AGAINST
## A BEAR HUG
## AND A FRONTAL ATTACK

(1) As assailant **A** bear-hugs Lee, pinning his arms, assailant **B** prepares to swing at him. (2) Lee counters with a left front kick to his groin. (3&4) He then places his

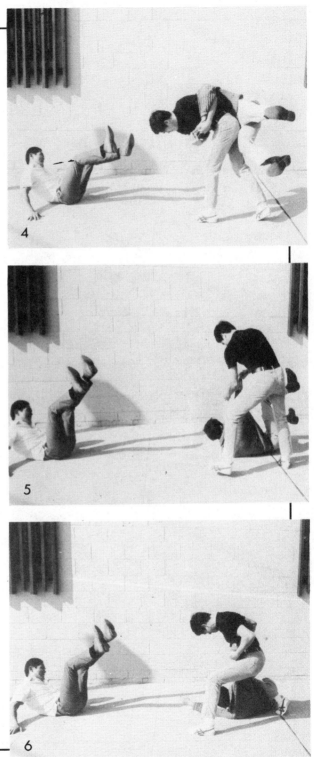

left foot back, holds assailant **B**'s arms and flips him to the ground with a twist of his body. (5 & 6) He finishes him off with a straight punch to his face.

## DEFENSE AGAINST A BEAR HUG AND TWO FRONTAL ATTACKS

(1) Lee is pinned in a bear hug by assailant **A**, as assailants **B** and **C** prepare to move in. (2) Lee quickly attacks the groin of assailant **A**. (3&4) With one sweeping

motion, he throat-chops assailant **A** with his left arm and punches assailant **B** with his right. (5) He finishes off assailant **C** with a side kick to his chest.

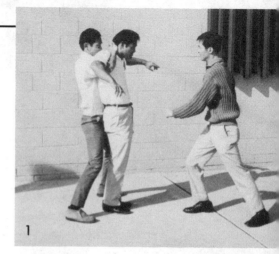

1

## DEFENSE AGAINST A FULL NELSON AND A FRONTAL ATTACK

(1—3) As you are held by a full nelson, assailant B moves toward you. Leaping high in the air, you kick the chest of B, causing him to reel backward. (4&5) As you land on your feet, bend forward and raise your right foot, slamming it hard at assailant A's instep. (6&7) As he loosens his grip, counter with an elbow to his face.

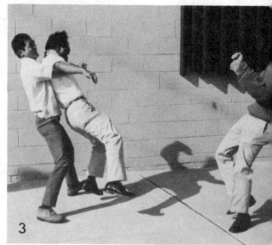

3

6

111

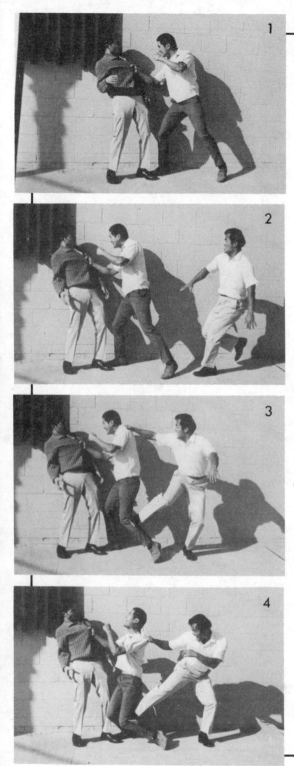

## AIDING A VICTIM OR FRIEND

(1) A friend is being shoved around by a bully. The bully has not seen you, so you quickly sneak up on him (2&3), grab his shoulder and deliver a side kick behind his knee, bringing him to his knees (4&5). Then both of you grab his wrists (6—8) and pin him to the ground with his face down.

*COMMENT: When two or three individuals attack you, they normally are overconfident and attack reck-*

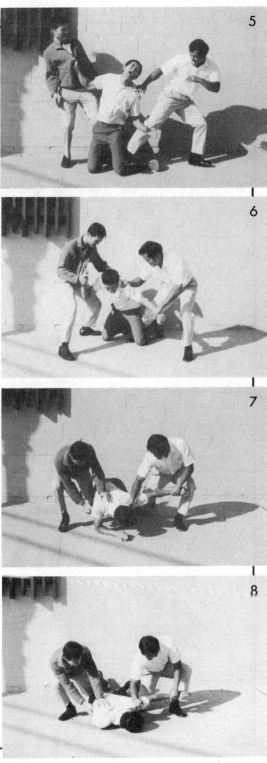

lessly. *This is an added advantage to you because they are bound to leave an opening for you, which they normally wouldn't on a "one-to-one" basis. Because you do not usually have a second chance against a multiple attack, you have to be sure that your techniques are executed with effectiveness. You can't worry about trying not to maim your assailants. You have to give all you've got.*

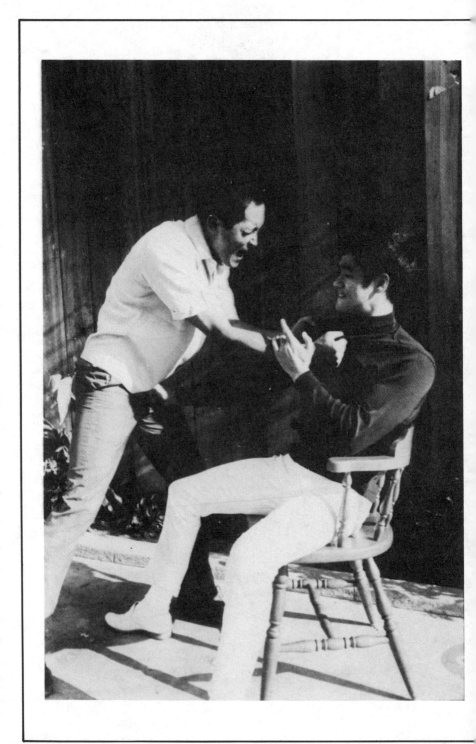

## CHAPTER VII

# DEFENSE FROM A VULNERABLE POSITION

Bruce Lee has included this chapter because he felt that an attack can come from anywhere even while you're sitting in a chair or lying down. Or you could be surprised and have to fight your way from a prone position or from being pinned on your back.

To Lee, any defense is all right—your delivery of kicks or punches doesn't have to be beautiful or picturesque. In self-defense, everything goes—scratch, bite, pinch, etcetera—any way to get out of a predicament without damaging yourself.

## DEFENSE FROM
## A CHAIR - FRONTAL ATTACK, No. 1

(1) Sitting in a chair, Lee is approached by an assailant. (2&3) Without warning, assailant rushes him and Lee instinctively delivers a front thrust kick to the groin without getting up.

## DEFENSE FROM
## A CHAIR - REAR ATTACK

(1) Lee, sitting in a chair, is surprised by an assailant from the rear who applies a headlock. (2&3) Lee grabs his hair and applies a finger jab to his eyes.

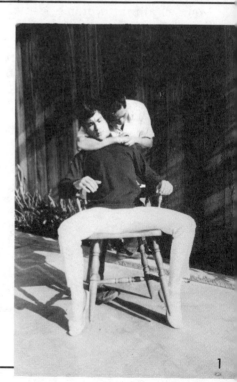

2

3

2

3

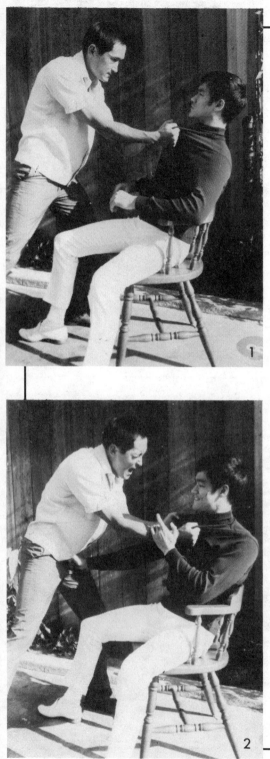

## DEFENSE FROM
## A CHAIR · FRONTAL ATTACK, No. 2

(1) While sitting in a chair, Lee is surprised by an assailant who grabs his shirt with both hands. (2) Lee quickly counters with a right punch to his groin.

COMMENT: *To apply your techniques in all these attacks, you have to be quick and effective. You are in a disadvantageous position, and a slow reaction on your part may mean further problems. For instance, if the attacker is able to knock you down from the chair and pin you, you have to apply other techniques which are not as simple and it may take longer for you to free yourself or incapacitate the assailant.*

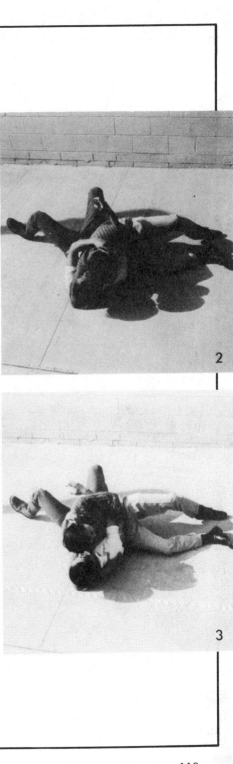

1

2

## DEFENSE FROM
## A LYING POSITION - HEADLOCK

(1) You are pinned by an assailant who has a headlock on you and has your right hand pinned. (2—4) With your free left hand, grab his ear and pull it until he releases his grip.

3

4

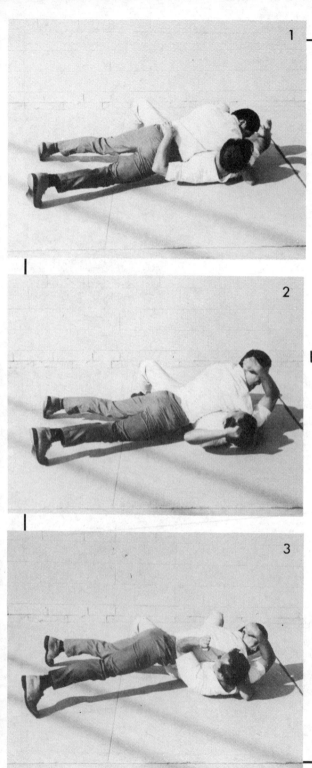

## DEFENSE FROM A
## LYING POSITION - CROSS BODY

(1) The assailant pins you with a cross body, leaving your arms free. (2&3) Grab his ear with your right hand and apply an elbow blow to his body.

## DEFENSE FROM A
## LYING POSITION · CHOKE

(1) You are lying flat on your back with the assailant squatting astraddle your chest, choking you. (2) Grasp one of his wrists to relieve the choke pressure and with your other hand apply a finger jab to his eyes.

*COMMENT: Defending yourself in the prone position is more difficult than from an upright position. First, you are not as mobile; second, you are limited in using all your defensive techniques like kicking or punching; third, because of your limited mobility, you can easily be overcome by two or more attackers.*

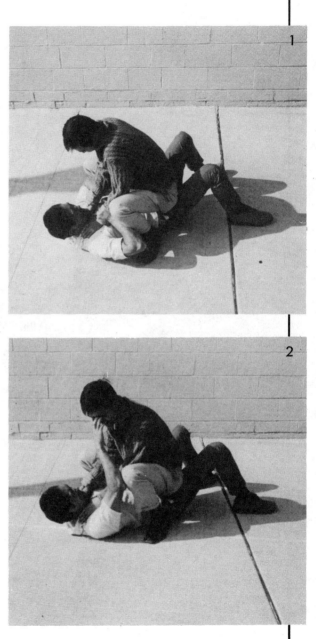

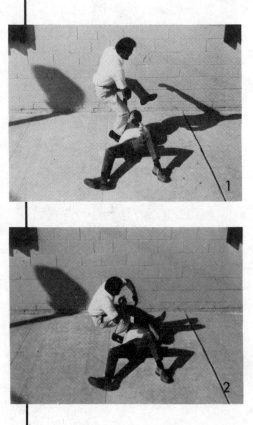

## DEFENSE FROM A
## LYING POSITION · STOMPING BLOW

(1) You are lying on your back and the assailant, holding your right wrist with both hands, attempts to stomp your chest. (2&3) Roll quickly to-

ward the assailant and trip him to the ground. (4&5) Then apply a left corkscrew hook to his groin.

# More Bruce Lee Books from Ohara

## TAO OF JEET KUNE DO
*by Bruce Lee. Code No. 401*

## BRUCE LEE'S FIGHTING METHOD Vol. 1: Self-Defense Techniques
*by Bruce Lee and M. Uyehara. Code No. 402*

## BRUCE LEE'S FIGHTING METHOD Vol. 2: Basic Training
*by Bruce Lee and M. Uyehara. Code No. 403*

## BRUCE LEE'S FIGHTING METHOD Vol. 3: Skill in Techniques
*by Bruce Lee and M. Uyehara. Code No. 404*

## BRUCE LEE'S FIGHTING METHOD Vol. 4: Advanced Techniques
*by Bruce Lee and M. Uyehara. Code No. 405*

## CHINESE GUNG FU
*by Bruce Lee. Code No. 451*

## THE LEGENDARY BRUCE LEE
*by the Editors of* Black Belt magazine. *Code No. 446*

## THE BRUCE LEE STORY
*by Linda Lee. Code No. 460*

## THE INCOMPARABLE FIGHTER
*by M. Uyehara. Code No. 461*

OHARA █ PUBLICATIONS, INC., 24715 Ave. Rockefeller, P.O. Box 918, Santa Clarita, CA 91380-9018

# LITERARY LINKS TO THE ORIENT